The Boy in the Box

Saving Remy

Stefanie Billette

Take Back Your Body LLC
North Carolina

Take Back Your Body LLC
North Carolina
www.TakeBackYourBody.com/books

Publisher's Note: This is a work of non-fiction. Names, characters, places, and incidents are real and accurate, unless otherwise indicated. Locales and public names are also real, unless otherwise indicated.

Ordering Information: Special discounts are available on quantity purchases by corporations, associations, non-profits, and others. For details, contact the publisher at Stefanie@TakeBackYourBody.com/.
Stefanie Billette — First Edition
ISBN 979-8-218-62152-0
Printed in the United States of America

Dedication

I dedicate this book to my brave son, Remy, and to all rare and undiagnosed children and their families. Our love will light the path.

Author's Notes

Half of all proceeds from the sale of this book will be donated to the National Organization for Rare Diseases (NORD). If you would like to contribute directly to the health and well-being of people with rare diseases to advance care, research, and policy, please visit www.rarediseases.org

The names of most physicians mentioned in this book have been changed. Many of the physicians we encountered failed us during Remy's medical crisis and would likely seek retaliatory action if I used their actual names. Therefore, I have created pseudonyms for those practitioners. The exceptions are the three doctors whom I credit with helping to save my son. I have used their real names: Dr. Anthony Perszyk, Dr. Erick Hernandez, and Dr. Thomas Searle.

I have also changed the name of "the school" and its administrators. Read on to find out why.

No disease that can be treated by diet should be treated with any other means
—Maimonides

Contents

Introduction

Inborn errors of metabolism (IEMs) affect up to 1 in
2,500 newborns. These disorders can be caused by inherited or spontaneous (de novo) mutations. They are a
large group of rare genetic conditions that prevent the
body from properly converting food into energy. IEMs
are usually caused by defects in specific proteins (enzymes) that help break down (metabolize) parts of food.
This defect can lead to a buildup of substances such as
amino acids and sugars which can damage organs and
cause a range of symptoms.

Each individual IEM is rare, but collectively, they are
more common than one would think. IEMs can be difficult to diagnose because their clinical presentation is often nonspecific. Several IEMs are now included in
newborn screening programs, which can help with early
diagnosis. While early testing can identify some

disorders, not all of them are part of newborn screening tests. Once an IEM is diagnosed, treatment is tailored to the specific disorder and can include specialized diets, supplements, and medications. The goal of treatment is to minimize or eliminate the buildup of toxic metabolites while still allowing for growth and development.

There are many types of inborn errors of metabolism, including Hereditary Fructose Intolerance (HFI), Glycogen Storage Diseases (GSDs), Phenylketonuria (PKU), and Maple Syrup Urine Disease (MSUD).

Primary mitochondrial disorders are a group of highly variable and heterogeneous inborn errors of metabolism resulting from defects in cellular energy, and these disorders can affect every organ system of the body.

CHAPTER ONE

The Neonatal

Intensive Care Unit

The NICU saved my son's life. But it also nearly killed him.

Remy was born seven weeks prematurely, weighing only two pounds, eleven ounces. Despite my dream of having a vaginal birth after caesarean (VBAC), I had to deliver Remy via C-section at thirty-three weeks because he stopped growing at twenty-seven weeks. Ultimately, it didn't matter to me how he came out as long as he was healthy.

Remy came out with his arms up, in a boxer's stance. It was as if he knew he would be in for the fight of his life—a fight even more difficult than the one he had in the womb.

"He looks great. His Apgar is nine and nine!" cheered the staff pediatrician, Dr. Elliot West.

I breathed a sigh of relief. As my obstetrician began to sew me up. I thought to myself, "My baby boy is healthy! Wow, those shots of betamethasone[1] must have really worked these past two days!"

"He weighs two pounds, eleven ounces." Dr. West continued.

I thought my daughter, Rebecca, had been tiny, weighing in at only six pounds, six ounces!

Shane learned from my first C-section that he should not look over the curtain during the operation. He was a bit traumatized after making that mistake during Rebecca's birth. This time, he kept his eyes on the doctor. I, on the other hand, could only see the ceiling. But I could hear the beautiful cry of my baby boy!

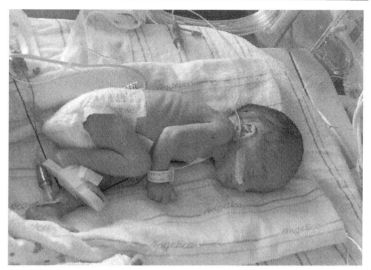
Remy, shortly after birth

Dr. West briefly brought my tiny preemie, who fit in his palm, close to my face so I could kiss him on the cheek. That was the only contact I would have with Remy for a while. Premature babies struggle to regulate their body temperature, so they are placed in tiny plastic boxes called incubators. Without an incubator, premature babies would waste their energy trying to stay warm and could develop hypothermia, which can lead to breathing problems and low blood sugar.

I was shaking uncontrollably. I had one of my Raynaud's attacks during the C-section, just as I had with Rebecca. With Raynaud's, a mysterious vascular condition, my fingers and toes turn white, my body starts shivering, and no quantity of heated blankets can warm me.

C-sections are very bizarre. I don't know why anyone would choose to have one. You have just enough feeling to know you are being cut open but not enough feeling to actually move. I certainly hoped I would not need to have one, but I ended up having two. My amniotic fluid was so low with Rebecca at 39 weeks that we had no choice. Remy was severely growth-restricted in the womb, so again, there was no other option. The difference was that Rebecca made it to full term, and Remy hadn't grown since the sixth month of my pregnancy.

As soon as my doctor "put me back together," I was taken to a room where my husband, Shane, was waiting for me. An hour later, Shane wheeled me into the NICU to see my precious little boy. There was my tiny son, in his plastic box, with an IV in his head and an NG tube[2] in his nose.

Remy's incubator had one tiny hand-hole on the side through which we could touch him (after thorough hand-washing at the scrub stations housed within the NICU). Shane is a big guy, and his large hands could barely fit through the tiny hand-hole to stroke our baby boy's delicate fingers.

All my life, I have tried to control everything. I liked being in charge. I liked running the show. The moment I saw Remy—so small and so vulnerable—I instantly realized what little control I had over anything. This miniature human being, with whom I had already fallen in love, was at the mercy of both his fate and his physicians instead of being cradled in my arms as I had hoped and planned.

I knew that the only thing I could give him that no one else could was my colostrum. I knew that this would give him the best chance of growing strong so that he could come home with us. Pumping colostrum would give me a purpose while I alternated between fidgeting in bed and pacing in my spacious, but empty, maternity suite.

Remy was immediately put on TPN[3], but I wanted to start giving him my colostrum as soon as possible. "Let the pumping begin," I thought as they wheeled me back to my room.

I am a very pragmatic person, so I was able to push aside any disappointment, sadness, and fear at that moment, because I had a job to do. But, as I pumped, I also worried about my daughter who was almost seven years old. She was the center of our world as an only child for so long, and in an instant, all my attention had to be given to someone no bigger than a banana.

Remy was a bit of a surprise....

Shane and I met when we were sixteen years old, but we lived three hours away from each other. We maintained contact even when we went to different universities in different states. After college, I took an analyst position outside of Washington, D.C. Shane reached out to me to say he loved me and that it was time for us to be together. Within a few weeks, he had moved into my apartment, and we were engaged. The next year, we moved back home to Florida, got graduate degrees, bought a house, became teachers, and decided (at age twenty-six) that it was time to start a family.

I lost identical twins and then miscarried another baby before we had Rebecca. I lost my fourth baby when Rebecca was four years old. We had all but given up on having a second child, but we weren't exactly doing a good job of preventing it. When we found out that I was expecting again, we were filled with mixed emotions. We were now thirty-six years old, much older than we were when we had Rebecca, and we were not in a great financial situation, living on two teachers' salaries. We had spent all our savings so that I could stay home with Rebecca for her first two years, and we never quite caught up.

When I made it past the first trimester, I breathed a sigh of relief. When we had our ultrasound to see the sex of the baby, Rebecca asked if there was any possibility that the sonographer was pointing to an oversized nose instead of the clear indicator of his biological sex. She really wanted a sister.

The second trimester of my pregnancy was uneventful, although I did have to go in for monthly appointments with a maternal-fetal specialist since I was considered high risk due to my advanced age and my history of miscarriage. I had frequent ultrasounds which had been excellent for months. However, once they saw Remy's growth slowing at twenty-seven weeks, I went in weekly. At thirty-three weeks, I was told he had barely grown in six weeks, and he had to come out or he would not make it. They gave me steroid shots, and we scheduled a C-section for the next day. I had asked my obstetrician if I should switch practices since hers only had privileges at our small local hospital, which had a Level 1[4] NICU, but she reassured me that everything would be fine and that she had delivered small babies before. During my entire pregnancy with Remy, just as I had with Rebecca, I sang "You are my sunshine" every single day. The day before Remy was born, I sang it to him, but this time, I followed it with a tearful prayer.

After Remy was born, I had to trust that Shane and my mother, Jennifer, were giving Rebecca the care she needed while I was at the hospital. In the NICU, I pumped eight times a day and was given only one hour per day to hold Remy. He could not be out of the incubator for more than an hour without risking hypothermia. Nurses skillfully cared for Remy all day long by putting their gloved hands through the tiny hand-holes on either side of his plastic box.

Skin-to-skin contact is so crucial to a NICU baby's development, especially when they spend twenty-three hours per day in a box. An hour of cuddles per day didn't feel like nearly enough time to hold my sweet boy, but my longing was quickly replaced by fear.

"His crit[5] is very low", said Dr. West. "He needs a blood transfusion."

I was shocked. How could he be anemic??? He was only a few days old! It didn't matter why, though, because he was pale and his bradys[6] were frequent. We were not in a children's hospital, and I was starting to think we should transfer him. We decided to get the blood transfusion first and then move him to a Level 3 NICU. I asked for a tour of the hospital's blood bank and was comforted, but I was still concerned since this was only the second blood transfusion they had ever done at this Level 1 NICU!

I began to do my usual online research. Time was of the essence, so we gave the go-ahead for the transfusion. It took longer than it was supposed to, but he came through it without any obvious problems. I casually asked for confirmation that the blood had been irradiated[7], because I had read about this on the NIH website while the transfusion was taking place.

"No, we did not think it was necessary," Dr. West told me nonchalantly.

I was confused and terrified. I had read that very-low-birth-weight babies (i.e., under 1,500 g) should be given irradiated blood, and Remy was only 1,200 g. The risk of graft-versus-host disease in premature infants is low, but if it occurs, it is fatal.

I started to sob as I read that it can take thirty days for symptoms to begin. I imagined the next month, watching my little love in an incubator as he struggled to grow, all the while fearing that he could die from the transfusion that was supposed to save him!

The doctor's reassurances did not help. The more questions I asked, the more I got the idea that they did not irradiate the blood because they had never transfused a newborn so tiny. A few hours after his transfusion, Shane and I agreed that we needed to transfer Remy to a Level 3 NICU. It was late, but I demanded that we move right away.

We moved via a NICU transport ambulance. I had no appetite, but I knew I had to eat if I wanted to produce milk for Remy. When we arrived at the Level 3 Children's Hospital (which was forty-five minutes from home), I realized that we were now small fish in a very big pond. We waited in a room with many other incubators until we were finally told there was a spot on the main floor. Remy's incubator was wheeled into a tiny cubicle that was separated from the others by a curtain. There were various alarms going off constantly, and it was impossible to relax. Being very germ conscious, I organized my breast pump components on the small counter space only after I wiped it down thoroughly. I washed Remy's pacifier, which had been rolling around in his plastic box on the ride to the hospital (babies in the NICU get pacifiers immediately after birth to provide comfort since they get such little human contact).

We had no family living nearby, but my mom had driven four hours to stay with our daughter at home while Shane and I spent the first week in the NICU nearly 24-7. Now that we were at a children's hospital, we were not allowed to stay there overnight, but we were told we could call anytime during the night to get updates.

"I want to stay here with Remy," I told Shane as I wiped away a waterfall of tears.

"I know," Shane said with sympathy. "But you need to come home to eat, shower, pump, and sleep. You can come back first thing in the morning. We brought him here so you could trust that he would be in good hands, right?"

I left enough breast milk to get Remy through the evening. I would have to continue pumping every two hours throughout the night and come back first thing in the morning to make sure he had enough tomorrow.

It was 1:00 a.m. by the time we got home. One would think I could have drifted off immediately from sheer exhaustion, but instead my mind overpowered my body.

"What if he develops Graft vs. Host?"

"What if he needs another transfusion?"

"How is Rebecca going to handle having me away all day?"

I finally fell asleep, but the alarm on my cell phone went off at 4:00 a.m.

Time to pump.

Shane got up with me and helped me wash the pump parts as I labeled and stored my milk in the refrigerator.

We went back to bed, and at 6:00 a.m., the alarm woke us up again.

"Pumping time," I muttered in a semi-conscious state as I stumbled down the stairs and into the kitchen. I still was not used to waking up to an alarm and a plastic breast-pump instead of my sweet baby boy crying for me.

It was time to get Rebecca up for school and Shane out the door for work. My mom had been staying with us since the day after Remy was born. As an only child, she and I were always very close, and she did not hesitate to leave her life to come help us. She and Rebecca had a great relationship, so Rebecca was happy despite my sudden absence. My mom would drop Rebecca off at school so I could go to the NICU and spend the entire day there. I would come home in the late afternoon and spend a couple of hours with Rebecca and eat dinner. Then Shane and I would head back to the NICU together for a few hours in the evening while my mom stayed with Rebecca. Entering a NICU is a surreal experience. Before reaching the babies, each visiting family member approached a large sink. There were individually wrapped sponges with an abrasive side and a soft side. There was a timer that counted down for two minutes as we scrubbed every surface of our hands to ensure that no germs were brough into the unit. We would wear masks until we reached our baby, and it was understood that no one would enter the NICU with so much as a sniffle.

After a week of evaluations by every pediatric specialist, the consensus was that Remy would need another transfusion very soon. They said that once a child is in the NICU, there are so many labs drawn every day that it is easy for their counts to drop. Since he had a transfusion shortly after birth, his body's production of red blood cells halted. His reticulocyte count[9] would be low for a while until his body recognized his increased demand.

The irony was that, as soon as a transfusion was done, the reticulocyte rate dropped because the bone marrow said, "OK, plenty of red blood cells now. Halt production," and so the cycle continued. In essence, blood was being taken from him faster than it was being made, so he was primed to become anemic again. Until the incessant blood draws stopped, I feared Remy would be on a never-ending loop of transfusions.

That week, Remy had his second blood transfusion at only three weeks of age. I felt relieved to find out that, at this children's hospital, irradiating blood was the standard for all NICU transfusions.

The problem was that Remy was still growing slowly, and he had begun regurgitating frequently. His labs were starting to reveal several abnormalities with his liver function and bone health.

He had high bilirubin[10], low albumin, very high alkaline phosphatase[11], high transaminases, low Vitamin D and many more "out of range" values.

One day, when my husband and I were home for our brief time in the evening, we began to cry and prayed that God would let us bring our baby boy home.

"Please don't let him die in the hospital," Shane pleaded.

We were exhausted and scared. But the NICU has a way of giving you the gift of gratitude. The next day, I was humbled as I watched other babies in the NICU struggle to breathe, undergo multiple surgeries, and eat through G-tubes[12].

There was a little girl next to Remy who never had any visitors. I was there sixteen hours a day and had never seen one person by her side. She looked very ill, and it broke my heart to see her all alone. One night, Remy's nurse, Courtney, told me her story.

"She was left here by her parents right after she was born. She has no family. We will take care of her until she is healthy enough to be placed in foster care and eventually gets adopted...if she gets healthy enough."

There was another baby who died while we were on the floor. The nurses cried briefly but had to move on to care for the dozens of other babies under their charge who needed to be fed, changed, poked, prodded, and cuddled.

When Remy was thirty days old, I finally took a deep breath. The risk of graft-versus-host had finally passed. And, when Remy turned seven weeks old, we celebrated because he hit the coveted four-pound mark. This is when a NICU baby can fit in a car seat and go home, provided s/he is healthy enough to do so.

Despite "making weight," the endocrinologists, gastroenterologists, and hematologists[13] were still concerned about his labs. I argued that his health would improve at home with his family. I convinced the staff pediatrician to release Remy with the promise that I would follow up with each specialist in the next week.

We put our baby boy in his infant car seat, which looked like it was going to swallow him, and for the first time, the four of us headed home together.

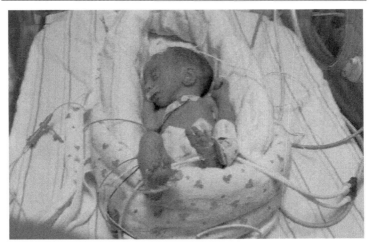

Remy at two weeks old (he was too tiny for us to call him by his
full name, Remington)

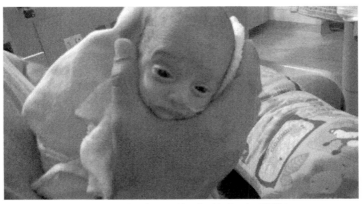

Remy, getting burped by Daddy in the NICU

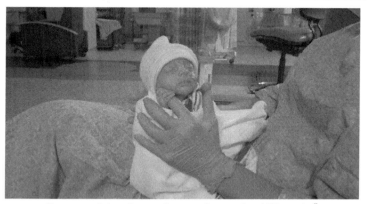

Remy, receiving therapy from an Occupational Therapist[8]

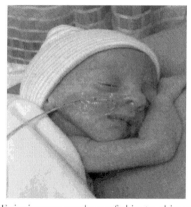

Remy & Me: Enjoying our one hour of skin-to-skin contact per day

Remy at four pounds and seven weeks old

CHAPTER TWO

The Search

Over the next eighteen days, we tried to get into a routine. Shane went to work, Rebecca went to school, and I stayed home with Remy. My mom drove four hours south to her house, intending to come back up after a few weeks. I spent the days pumping milk, feeding Remy, and cleaning up the inevitable vomit that would come after each feeding.

I found it ironic that I, of all people, would have a child who vomited regularly. When I was 5 years old, I woke up early one morning, found my Flintstones chewable vitamins and ate the whole bottle. Poison control told my mother to give me Ipecac which induces vomiting. Ipecac was used in the ER to cause vomiting of a poison. I spent the next 12 hours feeling like I was going to die

Thankfully, most emergency rooms have stopped using ipecac in favor of activated charcoal, and poison control no longer recommends home use. Unfortunately, I was left with a lifelong association in my mind between vomiting and death.

Remy hardly slept, day or night, and I was surviving on adrenaline alone. Well, maybe not adrenaline alone. I started to drink one cup of coffee a day for the first time in my life just so I could make it through the day.

Remy did not look well. His eyes were becoming the color of a lemon. Just three weeks after being released from the NICU, our concern became too great, so we took him back to the children's hospital, and he was admitted to the Pediatric Intensive Care Unit (PICU)[14]. Once you are discharged from the NICU, there is no going back.

His liver enzymes were out of range. He was also anemic again and needed another transfusion. As expected, his hemoglobin and hematocrit normalized after he was transfused, but his other labs remained worrisome. The doctors said they had never seen alkaline phosphatase in the 3000s before. They said his elevated bilirubin was abnormal, and his stools were a worrisome color and consistency. His ammonia level was also elevated, and this could lead to brain damage if untreated.

They wanted to rule out biliary atresia[15]. He would need to be given phenobarbital to prepare for a HIDA scan, which would allow them to view his liver. We were nervous about the test, but they reassured us that it was safe. The next morning, the nurse gave Remy his first dose of phenobarbital.

My eyes were so heavy from lack of sleep, but my attention was fixated on Remy. I looked down at his little hands, and my heart dropped. They looked like little sausages! Within seconds, I noticed Remy's eyes swelling.

"Nurse, something is wrong!"

The nurse examined Remy who was now looking like a marshmallow with puffy eyes, inflated hands, and bloated feet.

The doctor rushed into Remy's room.

"I have never seen anyone allergic to phenobarbital. That is very rare," he said with surprise.

"So is our son, apparently," I replied impatiently.

Since Remy could not have any more phenobarbital, the HIDA scan would not be useful. A new gastroenterologist suggested we do "exploratory surgery" instead. Shane and I scoffed at this suggestion.

"We will not put our son under anesthesia for a scavenger hunt," we replied as we left the children's hospital and headed home.

We talked for hours with each other, our families, and our friends in the medical profession to figure out our next step.

After much research and discussion, my mother and I whisked Remy off to one of only two hepatologists[16] in Florida who was six hours away. Shane stayed home with Rebecca so they could continue some normalcy with work and school. I knew I would be missing both my daughter's seventh birthday and our tenth wedding anniversary, but there was no time to delay.

Dr. Erick Hernandez was brilliant and compassionate; he encouraged me to continue pumping breast milk while other doctors had suggested I stop pumping and put Remy on formula. There is no doubt Remy would have died had I not followed his advice. Remy's labs were not good. Of particular concern to Dr. Hernandez was Remy's elevated PT/PTT[17].

"Remy's PT/PTT levels are high which means he is at risk for a major internal bleed," Dr. Hernandez continued. "I believe all of these liver abnormalities are due to his severe growth restriction in the womb. I am putting him on ursodiol, lactulose, vitamin K, and Polyvisol. Vitamin K is a clotting factor that will help combat the elevated PT/PTT. Polyvisol will raise his hematocrit. Lactulose will bring down his ammonia, and ursodiol will help his bile ducts."

Remy had his blood drawn a hundred times since his birth twelve weeks prior, so he needed a fourth blood transfusion while we were at this children's hospital under Dr. Hernandez's care.

After the transfusion, I noticed Remy was very calm...

"He is too calm," I thought to myself. I moved closer to Remy and kissed his cheek. He was cold to the touch.

"Something is not right," I fearfully told my mom.

I called a nurse into the room.

"My son is not OK."

She glanced at Remy and immediately mirrored my alarmed face.

She checked his temperature.

95.8 degrees.

She checked his blood glucose.

36.

In the next two minutes, fifteen hospital staff members flooded the room and surrounded Remy. I broke down crying. One nurse put him under a heat lamp while another hooked him up to an IV. One doctor checked his vitals while two other people, who appeared to be administrators, were huddled and whispering with concern.

"Oh, God. My baby is going to die," I murmured with my hand over my mouth to stifle the wails that were battling to escape.

A nurse came up to me. "Remington is hypothermic and hypoglycemic. We are trying to get his temperature and blood sugar up before he goes into shock."

What followed was the longest twenty minutes of my life. I didn't know if I would ever hold my baby boy again. I kept asking myself, "Did I kill him by bringing him here???"

After what felt like an eternity, a doctor spoke. "OK. His temp is up, and glucose is stabilized."

I felt the blood flow back into my hands, feet and head. "How did this happen?" I asked myself, shaking.

Once everyone else had left the room, I approached the attending pediatrician.

"Why did he react this way to the blood transfusion?"

He said he would look into it.

An hour later, he came back and delivered another shocking blow.

"The blood was not warmed prior to his transfusion, so that could have contributed to his temperature dropping."

"How could you give him cold blood?"

"We did not think it was necessary to warm it."

This response was becoming all too familiar. My faith in hospitals was quickly waning, and once again, I felt a burning need to get Remy out of there and take him home where I could better protect him.

After three days in the PICU, Dr. Hernandez discharged Remy. We would continue to give him the "cocktail" that was designed to heal his sick liver, and I would continue pumping breast milk.

It had been an exhausting three months, but we were all hopeful that we were off the medical roller coaster and could start our life at home together.

Remy began to show signs of improvement over the next few months. We got him caught up on vaccinations, and despite his reflux, vomiting, diarrhea, and inability to sleep for more than an hour at a time, we were grateful he was not in the hospital any longer. He vomited so frequently that my instincts were telling me to feed him every two hours to ensure he was getting enough nutrition.

When he was seven months old, I had to stop pumping because my milk supply disappeared. We put him on a hypoallergenic formula, and he started to eat solids, one at a time. On these new foods, he began to show signs of distress beyond the usual reflux and regurgitation. He slept horribly, and I continued to feed him multiple times each day. I would hold him all night most nights, and if I put him in the crib, I would sleep next to him in the rocking chair to check on him. I would often find him in a cold sweat. I kept wondering if he was having a blood sugar issue. Sometimes, after he ate, it looked like he was waking from a coma. But his lethargy would immediately turn to energy once he ate, and the cycle would continue.

He never seemed content. He was always hungry, then in pain, then vomiting. He would scream in the car, and I knew it was more than just reflux. So, we kept switching formulas. He did not take solid foods easily. Rice cereal and oat cereal stayed down for the most part, but once we began introducing fruits and vegetables, he threw up even more than usual. Some foods (e.g. avocado), he rejected outright. He willingly ate bananas and prunes, but he immediately vomited them. I recorded every food and every reaction in the daily log that I had been keeping since the day he was born.

By the time he was eleven months old, his liver was quite enlarged, and he looked like he had a potbelly. His jaundice was returning, and his ultrasound showed "lesions" that looked like "nothing we've ever seen" according to local radiologists and gastroenterologists. Again, doctors kept saying "liver biopsy" and "exploratory surgery." Aside from the inherent risks of surgery, he would need to fast for twelve hours prior to surgery, which I knew he could not do.

"He cannot go even four hours without food", we insisted. But that was beside the point, because there was no way we would let him go under the knife.

The college where I taught full-time was holding my position for me, but I was on unpaid leave. With a million dollars in medical bills and only one teacher's salary, we were in dire straits financially. Downsizing and lowering our monthly mortgage, plus getting equity out of our home, would be the only way out.

We sold our beautiful two-story home. It was the home where Rebecca and Remy were conceived and brought back from the hospital, the first house we ever purchased, the place we had lived in for twelve years and had spent nearly every evening socializing with our neighbors in the cul-de-sac. We simply could not afford the mortgage anymore. So, we bought a small condo and sold most of our lovely furniture.

The stressors were taking a toll on us individually and as a couple. Rebecca could feel our tension. Thankfully, Shane had just been offered a school administrator position with slightly higher pay. I knew I had to decide soon whether I would try to go back or lose my faculty position. We had put a lot of medical expenses on credit cards. I had to go fight insurance companies for reimbursement and then negotiate with our credit card companies. Our perfect credit dropped for a year, but it was better than declaring bankruptcy.

Our new condo had carpet in every room which proved to be quite messy with an infant who vomited multiple times per day. The bottom level was the garage and laundry area, and all the living space was upstairs. One afternoon, I walked over to the kitchen and saw that the baby gate at the top of the steps was open!

I immediately muttered, "Where's Remy?"

I ran to the stairs and saw my little boy on the landing, twelve steps down. Miraculously, he was giggling. Thank goodness the stairs were carpeted!

Rebecca felt so guilty that she had left the gate open. After we took Remy to the doctor and he checked out fine, it reassured her, but she thought of Remy as her little baby, and I knew that all the events of the past year had given her tremendous anxiety. Her guilt quickly became my guilt.

By ten months old, Remy began to adamantly reject certain foods. He also had not started speaking and still had no teeth. I scheduled an appointment with a speech therapist who specialized in food therapy. She assessed Remy and determined he pushed food out with his tongue as he chewed. This was likely due to ten months of vomiting, the use of a pacifier, and constant reflux. In March 2015, I was driving him to one of his appointments with Rebecca also in the backseat. I was particularly exhausted because my own autoimmune disease had been flaring, so I was not feeling well at all. Remy started to gag as he often did, but this time, I turned and looked back for a split second instead of using my rear-view mirror.

CRASH.

AIR BAGS DEPLOYED.

I hit the car in front of me. We were at a red light, and I thought the light had changed when I looked back, but the car in front of me had not moved. I immediately checked on the kids who appeared unscathed, sans a tiny cut on Remy's chin from his seatbelt. My wrist was throbbing, because it had gone into the dashboard on impact. I had airbag dust on me. But we were OK.

My SUV was pretty banged up and undriveable. Shane drove over from work and, once he knew we were physically all right, we both realized that this was going to be yet another financial blow. This was the first time in my life that I had hit a vehicle, and the last thing we needed was an increase in our insurance premiums.

We decided I needed to try to go back to work. I contacted the pre-school Rebecca had attended and registered Remy for the Fall.

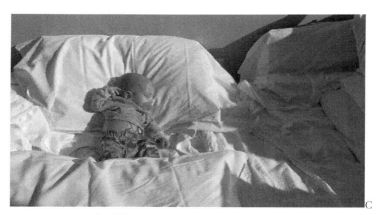

Remy, back in the hospital to prepare for a HIDA scan

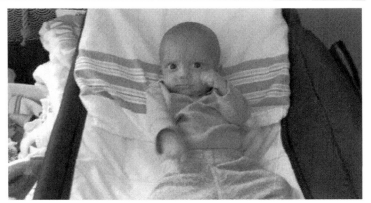

Instead of whining and feeling sorry for himself when he doesn't feel well,
Remy just gets downright mad. He was a fighter from day one

CHAPTER THREE

The Setback

In August 2015, I went back to my position as a college professor and Remy started pre-school. He was only one year old, so he was still in diapers. I packed foods that I hoped he would keep down, but every day, the teachers would hand me a report noting that he had foul poops, spit up, and stomach pain. I was thinking about him constantly at work and I knew that I wanted and needed to be with him. It was a long four months, and at the end of the semester, I formally resigned. Remy's teachers were sweet and loving toward him, but he was not well enough to be in pre-school. We still had no idea why.

When Remy was seventeen months old, we embarked on a journey that took us to multiple specialists. We took him back to Dr. Hernandez, who wanted to do an MRI. I was terrified of giving Remy anesthesia and also did not know how Remy would respond to eight hours of fasting. We checked into the hospital and waited. And waited. Then, a nurse came in and said the MRI machine was broken, and we would have to wait longer, which meant a longer fast. We took this as a sign and left the hospital. Dr. Hernandez called us and said he was sorry for the MRI problems and that he wanted to do whatever he could to help "our Remington". We told him that we appreciated him but that we would have to think about our next steps.

Over the next six months, we saw nearly every geneticist and gastroenterologist in Florida. Some would say, "Let's do a liver biopsy," but most would order more labs, which brought along the fear of Remy becoming anemic again. All the doctors had one thing in common; they all scratched their heads and said that nothing explained his unique array of symptoms.

One highly reputable geneticist stands out as the most disappointing. I lugged my briefcase full of records into her office with Shane by my side, carrying Remy. When Dr. Ella White walked in, she looked at Remy, then at her nurse and said, "Oh, that is an Alagille baby." At first, Shane and I felt a glimmer of hope when she uttered these words. But I had read about Alagille Syndrome, and Remy did not seem to fit the profile.

He had many symptoms that were not explained by Alagille, so I had to speak up.

"What makes you think he has Alagille?"

"Well, his dysmorphic facial features are a clear sign," Dr. White stated smugly.

It was true that Remy had the Alagille characteristics of a large head, low ears, large eyes, and a small nose and chin. But he was also severely growth restricted in the womb, vomited regularly, and was still classified as malnourished, none of which was explained by Alagille.

I hoped that she would dig a bit deeper. I spent two hours explaining and presenting Remy's medical history. She took copies of everything and said she would spend the weekend at home looking over all his labs, imaging, and progress notes and would call us after reviewing the piles of files.

We never heard from her. When I called her office, I was told she no longer had the time for our case.

At my annual ob-gyn check-up, I told my physician (who was educated in the UK) about Remy and his symptoms.

"Has anyone mentioned Glycogen Storage Disease?" Dr. Thomas Searle asked.

"No, what is that?" I was intrigued.

"GSD is a rare genetic disorder caused by enzyme deficiencies that can damage liver cells, cause poor growth, and lead to feeding difficulties as well as hypoglycemic episodes," Dr. Searle explained.

This sounded just like Remy!

I could not contain my excitement and gave Dr. Searle a huge hug as I left his office. I went home to my familiar NIH searches and began reading about GSD. I also read information about Hereditary Fructose Intolerance (a.k.a. Fructosemia)[18] which was similar to GSD but also explained Remy's elevated bilirubin. He had a few other lab results and symptoms that were not explained by either disease, but these two genetic diseases seemed to explain his primary symptoms.

Both GSD and HFI are treated through nutrition therapy. For HFI, the diet is 100 percent fructose-free. This involves much more than just eliminating fruits. Fructose is found in all fruits, vegetables, legumes, nuts, seeds, whole grains, spices, and sweeteners. Being fructose-free automatically means that one must be sucrose-free because sucrose is a disaccharide, which consists of fructose and glucose.

So, all "sweets" such as table sugar, honey, and molasses are off limits. There are also substances, such as sorbitol, which convert to fructose in the body and therefore must be avoided.

GSD Type 1 (the most common type) is treated by restricting fructose, sucrose, and lactose in one's diet and by drinking cornstarch mixed with water throughout the day to maintain normal blood glucose levels.

With both disorders, sugars get trapped in the liver and symptoms include an enlarged liver (hepatomegaly) and hypoglycemia.

Since I did not know whether Remy had GSD or HFI, I decided to treat him as if he had both! I gave him regular doses of cornstarch and strictly eliminated all the possible sources of sucrose, fructose, lactose, and sorbitol. Our little boy was now eighteen months old, and we were tired of having no answers.

A diet that is 100 percent fructose-, sucrose-, and lactose-free is difficult to maintain, to say the least. Sugars are everywhere. We live in a world where candy is thrown at children as a reward for answering math problems correctly. Sorbitol, fructose, and sucrose are in medications and vaccines. It took me a month of sorting through the wrong information from dietitians who knew nothing about HFI or GSD to finally get all the sources of these sugars out of his diet. We put him on a fructose-free and lactose-free amino acid formula that cost $1,000 per month, and I prepared all his food from scratch to guarantee they were safe. I became more and more convinced that he had HFI, but I decided to keep him lactose-free as well just to be on the safe side.

The change in Remy was miraculous. He immediately stopped projectile vomiting. He went from having no teeth to getting two or three teeth at a time. The acidic stools that caused severe diaper rash became a thing of the past. His hair grew. He began sleeping for more than two hours at a time. His hypoglycemic sweats nearly disappeared, and he was no longer yellow!

Clinical evidence confirmed what we were witnessing. Remy's belly shrank, and his labs improved. His ultrasound showed that those mysterious liver "lesions" were stable for the first time.

All of Remy's improvements were proof-positive that nutrition therapy was working. But he still ate like a bird and was nowhere near being in the normal range on the growth charts.

I have always been very organized, so in addition to the daily log I had kept since the day Remy was born, I created a recipe book so that in my absence, someone could prepare safe food for Remy. I always worried about what would happen to him if something happened to me. I went over everything with Shane, Rebecca, my mother, and my mother-in-law, Vickie, to make sure everyone knew how to keep Remy healthy.

◆◆◆

I had already made two medical appointments prior to putting him on the HFI diet. Without a diagnosis, how would we know the progression of his condition?

We went to a clinic in Pennsylvania at one of the top children's hospitals in the nation that specializes in rare diseases. We met with a team of experts who said they had never seen anything like this before. They all agreed something was not right, but they had no idea what it could be. They recommended genetic testing, and if nothing was found, they suggested a biopsy. They wanted to start with a few specific tests and would eventually get to more comprehensive (i.e., more expensive) tests. I wanted to test for HFI immediately, but they said that was not their first test. It would be months before we had results, and I would likely have to battle our insurance company to cover it, just as I had to fight for coverage of Remy's other medical expenses over the past eighteen months.

When we returned home, we saw a medical geneticist with whom I had made an appointment three months earlier. He was known for being a brilliant diagnostician who could solve the most complex genetic puzzles. We hoped he would have some theories while we waited for genetic results.

Dr. Anthony Perszyk was friendly, funny, and confident (but not condescending like so many of the doctors we had met before). He pored over my briefcase full of Remy's medical records and the daily food logs I had kept since day one. I gave him a summary of the journey we had been on the past year and a half.

"Are you in the medical field?" Dr. Perszyk asked.

I responded as I always did when asked this question.

"No, but I was pre-med and switched to psychology, much to my mother's dismay."

Dr. Perszyk was one of a handful of American doctors who was considered an expert in HFI, so I felt strongly that we were finally in the right hands. I told him about the restricted diet that we had started three months earlier. He was pleased that Remy's serious symptoms had abated, but he was concerned about his slow growth. In fact, Remy was still not on the charts. While he met many of his milestones, his verbal skills were lacking. He was still on bottles of formula for eighty percent of his nutrition, and he looked like he was half his age. Remy was getting all necessary nutrients from his amino acid formula, but Dr. Perszyk felt he needed more.

"I am putting him on Levocarnitine. This particular amino acid will improve his mitochondrial function and help him grow," Dr. Perszyk explained. "I want to see him back in three months to measure his growth and re-do his labs."

In the meantime, Dr. Perszyk agreed to order the test for HFI.

Six weeks later, the HFI test came back.

It was negative.

This did not make any sense to me. Remy's symptoms had improved markedly on the HFI diet.

Within a six-month period, we had many more individual genetic tests come back from the rare diseases clinic. All were negative. Next, the clinic ordered Whole Exome Sequencing (WES), a genetic testing technique that analyzes all the protein-coding regions (exons) of an individual's genome. WES also came back with no findings.

The experts at the rare disease clinic concluded that there was no need for Remy to continue on a restricted diet, since the tests were negative. My instincts told me otherwise, so I kept him on a carbohydrate-restricted diet and continued to give him L-carnitine.

We were baffled by the lack of a diagnosis. It was clear that the switch to fructose-free was helping. He was taking the amino acid formula and holding it down.

I ensured that all his food was "HFI safe," but his appetite was still low. After eighteen months of vomiting, food was not his friend.

There were some improvements. He was sleeping five hours straight at night for the first time ever. He was not in constant pain. He started to talk more. All of this told me that we had to be on the right track. I was certain that Remy could not metabolize fructose. I recalled one time, when he was only a year old, we gave him ibuprofen for his first fever, and he got so sick after taking it and looked like death. Children's ibuprofen contains sorbitol, which gets converted to fructose in the body and is seven times more toxic to the HFI liver than fructose. Surely, this experience was proof that he could not process fructose!

Genetic testing did reveal one thing. He was a carrier for GSD 1b. I asked the geneticists at the top major children's hospital if he could be a GSD 1b carrier who shows serious symptoms due to a combination of factors. While they said it is impossible for a carrier to be symptomatic, I considered the statistics.

Being severely IUGR due to pathology is rare.
Being Very Low Birth Weight (VLBW) is rare.
Having an allergic reaction to phenobarbital is rare.
Having an inborn error of carbohydrate metabolism is rare.
At this point, the word "rare" meant very little to us. Remy had been "rare" so often that nothing seemed improbable at all.

In search of answers, I joined the HFI message board, which is an excellent support group for those with HFI and their families. Like some others on the board, I relayed that my son had every symptom of HFI, yet genetic testing for HFI came back negative. I called the lead researcher for HFI in the United States, and after hearing Remy's story, he concluded that Remy may have an HFI mutation that is yet to be identified.

As I continued traversing a medical labyrinth with Remy, Shane left the school system to revive the family pool construction business. This meant traveling to his hometown nearly two hours away to work with his dad. Shane knew that he needed a career where there was no income cap so that he could continue to support our family while I cared for Remy. He would leave Sunday night and come home Friday night. My mom moved into the condo across the street to be of help to me and the kids with Shane gone all week.

One puzzle piece still didn't fit.

Most children don't get diagnosed with HFI until they start table foods or infant formulas that contain sucrose. Yet, Remy's liver symptoms started in the NICU while he was only on breast milk.

From the day he was born, I kept a daily journal, which detailed when and how much he ate, whether he got sick afterward, and how he looked and acted. My lifetime of recordkeeping was paying off as I started to see some patterns.

I had reiterated to doctors from the beginning that he gets hypoglycemic, to which they would reply, "That's because he's tiny." I always suspected that he was more than "just tiny."

"How did he develop jaundice and other liver issues as a newborn on breast milk in the NICU?" I kept wondering.

That is when the light bulb went off. "Was he given something else besides my milk?"

Then, I remembered that the nurses gave him a syringe of liquid every time they drew his blood. It was the method they used to calm the babies. I called the NICU manager where Remy spent six weeks and found out that the Sweet Ease® that is given to NICU babies is, in fact, pure sucrose. This realization sent my mind into a tailspin. The frequent dosing of sugar water explained his early fructose exposure and subsequent liver damage! I was even more convinced by this revelation that my little guy, indeed, had HFI.

The irony of this cycle hit me like a freight train. Our son had been given sugar to calm him for blood draws. As his labs worsened, more labs were drawn, and so he was given more sugar water!

I quickly launched a petition on Change.org to alter the practice of giving NICU babies sugar water by simply adding a warning label: "Stop administering Sweet Ease® if newborn develops signs of liver failure". This should be common sense since thousands of babies have undiagnosed metabolic disorders, and sucrose could pose great danger to them. Manufacturers of infant formulas have recently been pressured to remove sucrose from infant formulas, and the NIH is now connecting the dots between SIDS and underlying metabolic disorders.

I sent letters, along with my petition, to the manufacturer of the Sweet Ease®, the American Hospital Association, and even news outlets. As of this writing, not one of them has responded.

In the Spring of Rebecca's 3rd grade year, we decided it was time to move so that Shane would not have to commute, and our family could be together again. We left our friends and the coastal city we loved and had called home for over a decade. We rented a house and started a new life in the center of the state. Rebecca started at a new school with only a couple of months left before summer began. My mom sold her condo just as we did and found a new place to be near us once more.

By now, Remy and I were into our daily routine. Most of the days revolved around my making sure he was active but never at a deficit calorically. Every three months, Rebecca and I would take Remy to the children's hospital forty-five minutes away for a day of labs, ultrasounds, and playing with the colorful train set in the lobby. On one of those visits, Rebecca threw up right in the lobby. For once, my kid without the rare disease was sick while at the hospital.

Dr. Perszyk had discovered more than forty genetic diseases in his decades of practice, and he explained that we can only test for what we know. He always said that our son has something rare —so rare that it is possible no one else has ever had it or no one else had ever survived long enough to make it known.

Dr. Perszyk officially diagnosed Remy with "a defect in carbohydrate metabolism at the mitochondrial level with carnitine deficiency."

Mitochondria are the energy powerhouses of our cells. Fructose was depleting Remy's cells of ATP (cellular energy), so putting Remy on L-carnitine (which helps stimulate ATP) allowed his body to absorb nutrients and grow. At age three, he was finally on the charts for weight and height!

While his metabolic symptoms disappeared and he began to eat more solid food, he also started to have more frequent croup-like coughs. He gagged and vomited because he produced excess phlegm. I began to wonder if he had a compromised immune system.

One of the moms I had become friends with on the HFI message board told me her daughter not only had an HFI-like disorder (she, too, tested negative on genetic tests), but also had Eosinophilic Esophagitis (EoE)[20] triggered by wheat and dairy. Remy's eosinophil level had always been high, so she suspected that a wheat and dairy allergy was a plausible explanation for his chronic respiratory symptoms.

I eliminated wheat and dairy from Remy's already limited diet when he was four and a half years old. Within a few days, I noticed a dramatic improvement. Days passed, weeks passed, and months passed. There was no more wheezing, no more phlegm, and no more gagging!

Remy's medically restricted diet was working, as evidenced not just by his outward appearance but also by improved labs and ultrasound imaging year to year. He had labs so frequently that we were able to see dips and changes in his complicated chemistries that indicated his body was trying to heal but had relapses at times. Remy was no longer wheezing on a regular basis due to dietary allergies, but when he got a respiratory infection, he needed albuterol to help with his cough.

When he was ill with a fever, I would stay with him all night and feed him homemade chicken broth every few hours to keep him from experiencing nocturnal hypoglycemia. I researched endogenous fructose production, whereby the body produces fructose. This seems to happen under stress (e.g., illness). In most people, this would be a protective feature, but for Remy and others like him, endogenous fructose production could be dangerous.

I always noticed that on hot days (which was pretty much every day in Florida, especially living away from the coast), he would become depleted and lethargic at night and would have cold sweats while asleep. I was able to keep him hydrated even through some scary childhood illnesses. Hand, foot, and mouth disease hit him hard with a fever up to 104 and sores on his hands, feet, and in his mouth. I was scared that if I did not get enough calories in him, his liver would fail. After Remy had spent so many months in hospitals as an infant, my main goal was to keep him out of one.

When Remy caught rotavirus, it was nearly impossible to keep fluids in him. I made my own electrolyte solution for him, consisting of sea salt, water, and tapioca dextrose, but he would vomit that up along with his L-carnitine. He needed calories and L-carnitine or he could wind up in intensive care. We took him to the ER and asked for Zofran which helps suppress nausea. This allowed me to give him his electrolyte solution, homemade chicken broth, multivitamin, and L-carnitine until the virus passed. I was incredibly relieved and felt grateful when Remy asked if he could have some bacon after five days of vomiting and diarrhea.

His illnesses would wear me out even though I did not usually catch the actual viruses. With chronic lack of sleep and stress, my own autoimmune disease symptoms were worse than ever, and I knew I had to start taking care of myself. The stress of always worrying that Remy would end up back in the hospital had taken a toll on my body and my psyche. I decided at age thirty-nine to go on an anti-inflammatory/autoimmune diet. It was highly restrictive, but I was used to cooking for a restricted diet with Remy, so I knew I could do it. Remy and I ate a lot of meat, fish, and poultry. Our main carbohydrates were rice tapioca. Our fats came from animal protein and olive oil. I began to lose weight and feel great. Remy was gaining weight and feeling better.

Remy had a good appetite at this point, but he did not get excited about meals. I figured it was just the residual consequence of being so sick as an infant. I still disliked not having an answer, so I began to look for a connection with others who were undiagnosed.

I found out about the Rare Genomes Project, a program at Harvard, whereby participants' DNA (along with parents' and siblings') would be analyzed through Whole Genome Sequencing (WGS), the most comprehensive genetic testing available. WGS can help diagnose rare conditions and can help identify new genetic mutations linked to diseases. I applied to the program, and Remy was accepted. Shane, Rebecca, Remy, and I all swabbed our cheeks and sent our samples off to Harvard. I always joke that my children may or not get into Harvard, but at least their DNA was accepted.

The RGP genetic counselor told me that we might never hear from them again. "We only reach out if/when we find something".

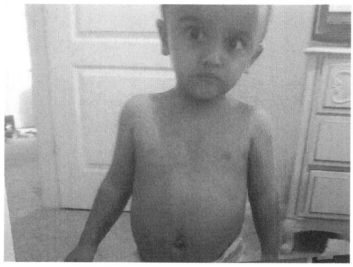

Remy, at age one, with a pot belly

Remy at sixteen months old

Remy, age four

CHAPTER FOUR

The School

At age five, Remy started accepting more "safe" foods
each day. I knew that, as he got older, he would be able to
communicate better, and a lot of the guesswork would go
away. I made him oat muffins and oat milk popsicles as
special treats, and he happily ate them while friends gob-
bled down cupcakes and ice cream at birthday parties. He
never complained. On some level, his body seemed to
know and told him, "That will make you ill."

Remy's diet at age five consisted of meats, fish, eggs,
and a few carbs such as oats and white rice. I calculated
his daily fructose intake and always kept it below 1 gram,
which was the threshold recommended for children with
HFI. I continued to operate under the assumption that he

had HFI even though there was no genetic proof yet. I made batches of pitas with tapioca starch, cornstarch, white rice flour, potato starch, eggs, sea salt, and olive oil. I prepared fructose-free, gluten-free, dairy-free pancakes, waffles, and bread. I always froze huge batches for him to make sure I could feed him if the power went out, which was very common in Florida. I procured safe beef, bacon, fish, and poultry to fill up my deep freezer.

After Remy had been home with me full-time for five years, we decided we would try sending him to school. I just didn't feel comfortable with him being at school all day without my being there to check on him. So, I decided to return to teaching. I applied to teach seventh/eighth grade math at the same school where he would attend kindergarten and where Rebecca would be a sixth grader. It had been a while since I taught middle school, but I was excited to get back to the classroom and hoped Remy would also have a great experience in kindergarten. Before the school year began, I spoke with his teacher and made it clear that he could only eat and drink what I sent in with him. I would check on him during my lunch break.

Dr. Perszyk said it would be safe to give Remy the MMR vaccine which protects against measles, mumps, and rubella. We had been waiting to give him live vaccines until his liver was functioning well for a long period of time. I was scared because the MMR contains a small amount of sucrose. I made sure Remy was healthy and that he had zero grams of fructose for the five days leading up to the vaccine. Thankfully, he handled the vaccine well and didn't have a severe reaction. I felt better knowing he was protected before starting school.

The first few months of school went very well. He was enjoying socializing, and I was enjoying working again. On one October afternoon during my planning hour, which was at the end of the school day, I went out to my car and brought a box back into the building. I turned into my classroom and immediately felt like someone was following me. I looked behind me, and one of my seventh graders, an awkward and quiet young man, was standing there staring at me. I asked him if he needed help with something, and without uttering a word, he reached his right hand out and grasped my right breast. I smacked his hand away and shouted, "No!" He ran out of my classroom and then out of the building as I yelled, "You can't do that!"

In my seventeen years of teaching, I had never experienced anything like this before. I immediately searched for an administrator. I found Mr. Tom Rumin, the assistant principal. I told him what happened, and he chuckled and asked "So, did he get to first base?" I found this disturbing, but my adrenaline was pumping so hard that I did not know what to say. He told me to find the ESE (special education) teacher, since the student who assaulted me was in special education. I found the ESE teacher and discussed the incident with her before I went home, assuming this would be handled appropriately.

My mom, upon hearing what happened, told me it was not safe for me to return to school. She is a psychologist and felt this was an early sign that this child could become violent. My husband wanted confirmation that the student would be permanently removed from my class before I returned to work the next day. I had not heard anything from the administration, so I called my principal, Mrs. Pukbuger, at 9:00 p.m. She told me that she did not have anywhere else to put the student, but that she could send in another adult to be in the room during his class with me. I asked what punishment he would be receiving, and she told me he would be suspended for two days. I asked about the psychological services he would receive, and she said she could not force that on him. I was also told that the cameras in the building did not show my classroom, only the hallway, so it was "his word against mine." She told me I should not file a police report.

Under the advice of a friend in law enforcement, I filed a police report anyway. The officer who came to the house to take my statement told me that I was doing the right thing. She had been assaulted by someone who was a repeat offender, and the first victim refused to press charges. She understood how I felt, and her encouragement provided me with some reassurance that I wasn't blowing the situation out of proportion.

The next few weeks were incredibly uncomfortable. I went from being a star teacher to someone with a target on her back. The school administrators began to harass me daily, questioning me on my lessons and insinuating that unnamed parents were not happy with me. One day, I was eating lunch at my desk with the door locked and closed, and someone knocked. I went to get it, but all I could see was a boy walking out of the building. I knew immediately who it was and went to tell Mr. Rumin that I was being stalked. He pulled up security footage and said the cameras were not working again. I asked him why that mattered when I was telling him exactly what had just happened. He ignored me.

I was so stressed after all that transpired that I came down with the flu. I would not send Remy to school without me there to check on him, so he was also absent for two weeks while I was home sick. Once I recovered, I returned to work and sent Remy back to class. His teacher said they would be having a field day outside with fun activities. I hoped this day would be a positive restart for both of us.

Later in the day, when I went to check on Remy, he told me he had thrown up because he had eaten silly string.

"WHAT?" I shrieked. I asked his teacher what had happened, and she said the kids were spraying each other in the face with silly string, and some got in his mouth. I was overcome with worry. What were the ingredients in the silly string? Did it contain anything toxic? Could there be sucrose or sorbitol in it?

I spent the whole afternoon and evening researching and talking to poison control. I felt that neither Remy nor I were safe at this school. I decided I would push through until the end of the school year, and then Remy and I would leave.

After the winter holidays, Mrs. Pukbuger came into my room during my planning period and told me it was time to part ways. I told her that I had no intention of returning the following year, but I wanted to be there to help my students finish the school year and to have Remy finish kindergarten. I had made such gains with the remedial math students who walked in hating math and were now writing songs about polynomials and volunteering to come to the whiteboard and teach their classmates.

She did not care. I told her I had never been asked to leave a job and always had administrators who wanted me back. She told me to resign. She said it would be "better for my career than being let go." I told her she would have to fire me and that I knew she was doing this as retribution for filing a police report against the student who assaulted me and refusing to sweep it under the rug as she had advised.

I called Shane and told him I was packing up my office. Remy and I left Rough River Charter School for the last time. Rebecca was still a 6th grade student there, and I prayed that the administration would not punish my straight-A, well-liked twelve year old daughter as payback.

I consulted with an attorney who told me a court case would be a long process, and it would be highly publicized in the small town we lived in. My husband grew up there and knew everyone. I did not want that kind of publicity, so I decided to leave the school, withdraw Remy, and move on with our lives. From that moment on, I knew that I would be homeschooling Remy. Little did I know, Rebecca would also be home with me for the next two years thanks to Covid. From March 2020 through March 2022, the kids, Shane, and I lived in isolation. Shane sold and built swimming pools while the kids did virtual school. I cooked, cleaned, and cared for my kids. I wrote health articles, books, and started my own line of autoimmune-friendly baking mixes. I coached those with autoimmune disease on how to change their diets and heal as I had.

We even got a pandemic dog. We saw friends and family outside but, for the most part, it was just the four of us day in and day out. Having our own pool made all the difference. Our backyard was a welcome sanctuary, with a lake, giant trampoline, swing set, and ample shade to keep us from melting in the Florida sun. The upshot was that we were spared the usual viruses and were all healthy during those years.

Shane and I got the Covid vaccine, but we did not feel comfortable giving it to either of the kids. Shane had a fever for a few hours after the vaccine but was fine after that. I, on the other hand, had an overreaction to the vaccine thanks to my autoimmune disease. I could not lift my arm for a week, I was in bed with fever and body aches for days, and I even had sore eyeballs (yes, you read that correctly). I reported my atypical reaction to the CDC.

In March 2022, we decided to venture out more and even removed our masks in most environments. Remy came down with a cold almost immediately. Thankfully, it was mild. I was relieved that his immune system was being challenged but not overly stressed now that we were out in the world again.

By age eight, Remy was starting to like food more. He understood that he could not eat "fruits, vegetables, or any form of sugar," as he says. In truth, he could consume very small amounts of fruits and vegetables in some combination on a daily basis, totaling less than 1g per day which equates to a few olives, a sliver of bell pepper, and a small orange wedge. Alternatively, he could eat ½ cup of kale, a small chunk of watermelon, and so forth, but not in the amounts that the rest of us are able to.

He used to say "food makes my tummy hurt" but, by age eight, he began to enjoy eating, and that made me so happy. Those early experiences stick with us, and it took a long time for him to trust any food other than his bottles of amino acid formula.

Remy was still not a deep sleeper even at eight years old. I believe the early days of NICU alarms and hypoglycemic episodes set the stage for poor sleep patterns. Once he turned five, he started sleeping through the night. But he still had restless nights. Remy would frequently get "head sick" (his words) around 5:00 p.m. He would complain of head pain, lie down, vomit, and fall asleep. I concluded these were migraines, induced not just by motion (he wore motion goggles in the car for that reason), but that these migraines were somehow triggered by stress, whether it be emotional, viral, or heat induced. Yet another diagnosis to add to the long list.

CHAPTER FIVE

The Decision

In May 2022, Shane and I decided that it was time to leave Florida. This was my second time moving out of Florida. I went to college in Virginia and vowed never to return. However, after the year living outside of D.C. and hydroplaning in a snowstorm, Shane and I had decided to return and settle down in Florida to be near our families.

Twenty-one years later, the heat in Florida became too brutal. It was not just uncomfortable, but unhealthy, especially for Remy. He couldn't play sports outside even though he was a natural athlete. Even with levocarnitine, he would get depleted easily. He tried to play tennis and soccer, but he would often become overheated, sweat profusely, experience stress-induced migraines, become hypoglycemic, and vomit. We needed to move somewhere cooler. Shane and his dad sold the family pool construction business and began acquiring land in the North Carolina mountains. Rebecca was about to start high school. It was the perfect time to make a big change.

Right after Remy turned eight, we moved to the mountains of western North Carolina. Remy's health improved instantly. The lack of humidity and cooler temperatures suited him perfectly. He hardly sweated and was able to play outside without crashing metabolically. His migraines were less frequent, but he still experienced nosebleeds in the wintertime from the dry air.

Rebecca began high school while Remy and I joined a community homeschool co-op. Shane and my father-in-law, who also wanted a change from Florida, spent their days turning raw land into buildable ten-acre lots with utilities and roads. My mom sold her house in Forida and rented an apartment near us. I continued to search for answers.

In December 2022, we flew to Miami. Since the Rare Genomes Project at Harvard had yielded no fruit (pun intended), I had applied to the Undiagnosed Disease Network (UDN) run by the National Institutes of Health (NIH), the largest study of the rare and undiagnosed in the world. Remy was accepted, and we all gave blood samples and sent them off to Baylor Genetics in Texas for Whole Genome Sequencing. Again, I was told we may never get an answer. Nevertheless, I was hopeful and made connections with others in "diagnostic limbo." Even though Remy was healthier than ever, I always worried that without a firm diagnosis, we would never know how his condition would evolve and whether there would be surprises down the road in his development.

Around this time, I realized Remy could tolerate whey and lactose, but not casein. This meant he could now eat butter and ghee but not milk and cheese. This expanded his menu options a bit. I also found a dairy-free cheese that Remy could eat (Violife). Much like his wheat allergy and his migraines, his casein allergy was a separate issue from his inborn error of carbohydrate metabolism.

Remy's diet became more varied. He could eat unsweetened cornflakes, white potatoes, popcorn, and other carbohydrates to balance out his animal protein-based diet. I always had him start a meal with protein and then follow it by carbohydrates, as the sequencing of food affects blood glucose levels.

Eating less red meat was a positive shift because Remy's creatinine level had been high due to his high protein diet. With more carbs in his diet, his creatinine came down. His Cystatin-C (a more precise measure of kidney function) was normal which meant his kidneys were healthy. His balanced diet also seemed to be working for his liver. At age eight, his liver enzymes were normal for the first time ever!

◆◆◆

We drove down to Florida for Spring Break 2023 during Remy's third grade year. Remy and Rebecca desperately wanted to visit Harry Potter's World at Universal. We obliged, spending a lot of time and money on both the experience and on two "magic" wands which still sit in boxes to this day.

The day we returned home, my throat felt scratchy. The next morning, I woke up with a headache and sore eyeballs. I immediately knew it was Covid. None of us had come down with Covid before. With my autoimmune disease in full gear, I was in bed with fever, aches, and sore eyeballs for forty-eight hours. My Raynaud's attacks were severe for the next few days, with my extremities turning white then purple.

I quarantined myself in the hope that I would not spread the virus, but a few days later, Shane, Rebecca, and Remy tested positive. Rebecca had no symptoms, Shane had mild flu-like symptoms, and Remy had a fever, pink eyes, and red cheeks. I researched and found that the latter symptoms were common in children with that particular Covid variant.

The most distressing event happened one evening when I woke up in the middle of the night. I went into the living room where Shane was watching TV. I started to feel lightheaded and the next thing I knew, I was on the floor opening my eyes to find Shane hovering over me asking if I was OK. As I later learned, I was fortunate that my singular syncope experience did not lead to POTS

(Postural Orthostatic Tachycardia Syndrome) which has become much more prevalent in association with Covid.

We all recovered relatively quickly from Covid symptoms and had labs drawn shortly after. Sure enough, Covid hits you where you are vulnerable. Rebecca's and my thyroid antibodies were sky high, and Remy's liver enzymes were up. It took three months for our labs to normalize.

I also lost my sense of smell and taste for a week while I had Covid. Perhaps it was my temporary lack of smell and taste that made me more acutely aware of others' ability to smell and taste. We had always known Remy had a weaker-than-normal sense of smell, but for the first time, I began to question whether he had a poor sense of taste as a result. He had never said anything about food having no taste, but how would he know what taste meant if he had never experienced it?

I wanted to know if Remy had hyposmia (a reduced sense of smell) and consequently, a dulled sense of taste or anosmia, a complete lack of sense of smell. I blindfolded him and did my own little experiment to test his senses of smell and taste.

When presented with a coffee-scented candle, Remy said he could detect a faint smell, but all other smells that we tested, including perfumes and various herbs, were indetectable to him. Likewise, with foods, he seemed able to detect "saltiness" and "spiciness" from cinnamon and black pepper, but he could not discern the taste of turkey from beef or rice cereal from oat cereal. While he could identify foods based on texture, it seemed flavors eluded him completely.

I took Remy to a pediatric ENT who ran a scope up his nose and could not find anything anatomically wrong as far as he could see. It would take an MRI to look further back. He said Remy's olfactory bulb likely did not develop fully in the womb. He also told us that his own wife has hyposmia and that it is more common than one would think. For a moment, we all felt so sad for Remy that, on top of everything else, he could not smell or taste. But then I realized that he has always been this way. It was not brought on by Covid. This is just who he has always been. To him, it is not a loss. It is just normal. I asked him if he still enjoys food, and he said, "Of course, mommy".

My main concern is safety. If he cannot smell smoke, how would he know if there were a fire? How would he know if food had spoiled? I concluded that he would have to rely on his other senses as well as smoke detectors and expiration dates to keep him safe.

In the spring of 2024, Rebecca developed a cough. It lingered much longer than her usual viral coughs. I took her to an internist who insisted it was viral and said it would pass. Her cough improved a bit, so we flew to

Florida for our niece's high school graduation. Rebecca's ears hurt so badly on the plane that she was in tears. I took her to urgent care and was told she had a double ear infection, which she had not had since she was little. She was put on amoxicillin. We got home, and her ears did not improve.

Then, Remy began to cough. As usual, I checked his temperature and oxygen. His oxygen saturation level (O2 SATS) had never gone below 95% even when he had respiratory viruses and had to use albuterol. This time, I saw his O2 SATs drop to 88% at night. I was getting worried. I took him to his pediatrician who again reassured me it was a virus, and he would get better.

A few days later, with Rebecca still coughing and Remy still with a fever, low oxygen, and looking pale, I took him back to see a different pediatrician. Around the same time, our friends found out that they had mycoplasma pneumonia (bacterial "walking" pneumonia). We spent a lot of time with the Condon family and realized that had to be it! I told the pediatrician, and she ordered a respiratory panel. We continued to give Remy albuterol, but it did not keep his oxygen up for long. The panel came back revealing that Remy indeed had mycoplasma pneumonia! This explained why Rebecca did not get better on amoxicillin. Penicillins do not work on M. pneumoniae!

We immediately got azithromycin (Z-packs) for Remy and Rebecca. Shane and I decided to put ourselves on it as well, even though we had no symptoms, because once someone in the household has it, everyone will eventually develop it. This was the first time Remy was ever on antibiotics. I don't love antibiotics and try to avoid them whenever possible, but in this case, it was critical. Remy's O2 SATS started to climb within twenty-four hours. Once again, my strong and brave boy didn't complain. He just got through it.

Shortly after we moved to North Carolina, Dr. Perszyk retired. Dr. Perszyk had been the one constant for nearly a decade. We needed to find a new geneticist who could be the point of contact in an emergency, physically examine Remy on a regular basis, and who could order regular labs and ultrasounds at a children's hospital to monitor Remy.

I took Remy to one of the most well-known Children's Hospitals in the nation, now located just a few hours from us. Remy and I met with the geneticist, and I brought him up to speed on Remy. He seemed disinterested once I mentioned that Remy was part of the NIH's UDN study.

He ordered labs, and a few weeks later, I received a message in the portal from him. "Remy's carnitine levels are normal, so he doesn't need to continue supplementation."

"WHAT?" I screamed.

This was the second time that a highly regarded researcher had told me to stop doing what had clearly been working for Remy. This logical fallacy is akin to a cardiologist saying, "Well, your blood pressure is normal, so you can stop taking your blood pressure medication."

I could only conclude that the geneticist we saw had no interest in caring for Remy because Remy was not someone he could add to his research studies.

Once again, I had to search for a new doctor.

I made an appointment with a different geneticist. He was unaffiliated with any research institutions, which meant his top priority was being a clinician and helping his patients. He was young and kind. Remy instantly loved him because they talked about Pokémon. We discussed labs and imaging. Remy had frequent abdominal ultrasounds to monitor the lesions on his liver which had been present since the NICU. I always opted for an ultrasound instead of an MRI since I did not want to put him under anesthesia. He asked if I thought Remy could lie still at this point, since an MRI would be more revealing. I decided I would train Remy to lie still. I bought a kids' play tunnel and would have him lay for ten, fifteen, and then twenty minutes at a time a few days a week, listening to music and remaining still to simulate an MRI. After two months of training, he was ready.

Just two days before we were to travel to stay overnight and undergo the fasting MRI, the radiologist said the MRI would be useless without a contrast agent. Gadolinium (Gd) is a contrast agent that is often injected into the bloodstream during an MRI to enhance the visibility of certain structures. Gd can remain in body tissues for several years after injection.

My mother, who has a brain aneurysm, would get frequent MRIs to monitor the aneurysm. She had a history of strong reactions to contrast agents including metallic taste, brain fog, joint pain, and skin reactions. I, too, had several brain MRIs to make sure I did not inherit an aneurysm, which runs on her side of the family. Gd caused a similar reaction in me. After having strong reactions, my mother and I switched to having our brain MRIs without contrast, which still offered valuable information. I had hoped Remy's MRI would also be illuminating even without contrast, but the radiologist insisted it was pointless to have an abdominal ultrasound without contrast.

While it would be nice to know more about his liver lesions than merely their size, Remy was doing well enough with stable labs and manageable symptoms that I was not willing to take chances unnecessarily. We scheduled an ultrasound once again.

Even after nearly a decade on a fructose-free diet with stable labs, the lesions on Remy's liver have not shrunk. This remains a mystery because, in theory, the liver should heal once the toxin is removed. However, I have talked with some other families of children with IEMs who also say their children still have liver damage despite improvements in symptoms and blood chemistry.

CHAPTER SIX

The Gene

In April 2024, just before Remy turned ten, the UDN sent a follow-up letter. They also called me to let me know that, after running Whole Genome Sequencing multiple times, they thought they may have found something. Remy has a de novo mutation on the ATF5 gene. The mutation was not inherited but spontaneously emerged during embryonic development. Shane and I were instantly amused by the tough-sounding name of the gene.

ATF5 is a protein-coding gene that regulates cellular differentiation, survival, and adaptation to stress. It plays a crucial role in the regulation of mitochondrial function and is expressed in many tissues, including the liver. ATF5 is associated with some cancers. We have always monitored Remy's tumor marker (alpha fetoprotein) since it was elevated when he was an infant. Thankfully, it has stayed normal over the years. ATF5 is also associated with olfactory development, which could explain Remy's anosmia!

UDN will continue to investigate this variant and look for other patients in the world who may have the same mutation and set of symptoms. We are hopeful that in Remy's lifetime, this particular variant will explain everything Remy has been through and, perhaps eventually, there will be gene therapy to target his genetic variant. I only hope that I will still be around to see it.

Remy is rare. He is, in fact, the rarest of the rare. I have met so many fantastic people being part of a network of rare kids and their parents. I have forged friendships with people who live across the country and across the world, most of whom Remy and I will never meet in person. While our stories are all unique, we share a common link of fear, love, perseverance, and hope. I write about Remy whenever and wherever I can so that we can connect with those like him and to let others know they are not alone and that there is an answer out there.

My first book was about nutrition and how eliminating certain foods saved Remy, turned my life around, and helped my daughter manage her autoimmune disease early on. Remy's story continued beyond the implementation of his restricted diet and that was the impetus for my decision to write this book.

Remy turned ten years old this summer. It has been a decade of immense worry and of profound love. Having a treatment that is working in the absence of a firm diagnosis is frustrating, but it is preferable to the reverse. We know that this is an unpredictable journey. It can be scary to not know exactly what his future holds.

I bring Remy's homemade foods, vitamin supplements, and compounded medications wherever we go. He wears a medical ID necklace to communicate his condition in case of an emergency. We need a kitchen wherever we travel.

Food is not the center of his life. He eats to live, not the other way around. That said, I want to do everything I can to make eating enjoyable for him. When Remy was four years old, I reached out to Chomps (https://chomps.com), a company that makes meat sticks. I had been enjoying their meat sticks for years and often wished Remy could have a convenient, shelf-stable form of protein to carry around in his backpack. In my email, I described Remy's condition and his restricted diet. They created samples and sent them our way. We gave them feedback, and they developed a meat stick that is safe for Remy in small quantities! I am so grateful to Chomps for giving Remy and children like him a safe, convenient source of nutrition.

I formed a group on Facebook called "moms of children with rare diseases". While there are FB pages for many rare diseases, I realized that there are many families like us who have an undiagnosed disease with a unique array of symptoms. I wanted to create a forum where we could connect, and maybe one day I will find another child who shares Remy's unique history and ATF5 variant. I currently have 150 members. We are all mothers who love our children and want them to lead the healthiest and happiest lives possible.

After a decade, we still don't know why fructose makes Remy so ill and why his liver lesions have not improved. His defect is likely in the mitochondria of his liver which is why L-carnitine has helped him so much. We do not know if his ATF5 variant explains every symptom he has had since before birth, but what we do know for certain is that he is strong, brave, happy, smart and active. He is loved beyond measure, and at age ten, he is able to understand what it will take to keep himself healthy.

Remy, enjoying a homemade saffron popsicle

Remy, age ten

[1] Betamethasone is a steroid given to mothers to speed up lung development in preterm fetuses who are at risk of being born too early.

[2] Naso-gastric tubes are used to send food through the nose directly into the digestive system.

[3] Total Parenteral Nutrition is commonly given to preterm infants immediately after birth until full enteral feeds are established.

[4] All hospitals have at least a Level 1 NICU, which offers basic newborn care. Level II offers more advanced newborn care. Level III offers a full range of pediatric subspecialties for critical care. Level IV offers the highest level of acute neonatal care.

[5] "Crit" is short for hematocrit, which is the proportion, by volume, of the blood that consists of red blood cells. Low hematocrit indicates anemia.

[6] Part of the NICU vernacular, "bradys" are Bradycardias, slowed heart rates that indicate distress.

[7] Irradiated blood has been treated with radiation to prevent Graft-versus-Host Disease which is caused by white blood cells called lymphocytes in the transfused blood recognizing the patient as "foreign", leading to severe illness or even death.

[8] Occupational Therapists in the NICU help reduce the stressful conditions that the premature or ill newborn is exposed to as a result of psychological and

physical immaturity. They help the newborn develop fine motor skills such as grasping an object.

[9] Reticulocyte count measures how fast red blood cells are made by the bone marrow and released into the blood. It rises when there is a lot of blood loss or certain diseases in which red blood cells are destroyed prematurely, such as hemolytic anemia.

[10] Bilirubin is an orange-yellow substance made during the normal breakdown of red blood cells. Bilirubin passes through the liver and is eventually excreted out of the body. High bilirubin may indicate different types of liver problems.

[11] Alkaline Phosphatase is an enzyme in a person's blood that helps break down proteins.

[12] A gastric tube is inserted directly into the stomach to provide nutrition to people who cannot obtain nutrition by mouth, are unable to swallow safely, or need nutritional supplementation.

[13] Endocrinologists specialize in hormonal and metabolic disorders; gastroenterologists specialize in organs of the digestive and elimination systems, such as kidneys, intestines, and liver; hematologists specialize in disorders of the blood and bone marrow.

[14] The Pediatric Intensive Care Unit is for children up to age eighteen.

[15] Biliary atresia is a rare disease of the liver and bile ducts that occurs in infants.

[16] A hepatologist is a sub-specialist in the specialty of gastroenterology who diagnoses and treats diseases of the liver and bile ducts.

[17] Prothrombin Time (PT) and Partial Thromboplastin Time (PTT) evaluate the overall ability to produce a clot in a reasonable amount of time.

[18] Hereditary fructose intolerance (HFI) is a metabolic disease caused by the absence of the enzyme Aldolase B. In people with HFI, ingestion of fructose (fruit sugar), sucrose (which includes table sugar) or sorbitol (which is converted to fructose in the body) causes severe hypoglycemia (low blood sugar) and the buildup of dangerous substances in the liver.

[19] EOE is an immune response that is usually triggered by certain foods or environmental allergens and causes GERD-like symptoms.

Epilogue

I used to be judgmental (OK, I still am to a degree). I used to think that when children had meltdowns, it was all the parents' fault. I used to think my daughter was well-behaved only because I was a loving and attentive mom. Having Remy taught me that there are so many factors that go into a child's early development.

Living in a plastic box and fighting for one's life does affect behavior and temperament. Similarly, going from an only child for six years to being forced to give up the spotlight for an ill sibling does affect a child's anxiety level and coping skills.

I am immensely grateful to the NIH and the researchers who are trying to find gene therapies. However, if we had waited for a precise diagnosis, a "cure", or a medical treatment, Remy might not be here today. It took paying attention to patterns, documenting everything, and looking for pieces of advice that made sense in order to discover nutrition therapy that would help Remy go from dying to thriving.

Nutrition can have a profound effect on anger, patience, and mood for both children and their parents. Very few physicians and psychologists will ever ask a patient about his/her diet. As a former teacher, I could tell you the moment my students walked into my classroom who among them had a nutritious breakfast and who grabbed a pack of Doritos and chocolate milk on the way out the door. I had many students who were labeled ADD/ADHD and regularly ate candies laden with food colorings, such as red dye 40, which has been shown to negatively affect cognition and behavior, exacerbating (if not directly creating) ADD/ADHD symptoms. Sadly, most parents look to pharmaceuticals to control ADD/ADHD symptoms instead of looking in their pantries.

Remy had frequent tantrums up until the age of four. I vividly remember a meltdown in the middle of Target's toilet paper aisle that easily could have been interpreted by others as evidence of "a bad kid" or "a lack of discipline." In truth, my son was in pain and did not know how to communicate it to us. It took a lot of detective work, love, and time to figure out why he behaved the way he did. I do think it is our responsibility as parents to find out why our children behave the way they do and to do everything we can to improve their physical and mental well-being.

It is easier in the short term to feed your body or your child's what is quick and convenient. But it will take much more time and energy in the long haul to manage the chronic diseases that follow. Beyond metabolic and autoimmune diseases, there are many conditions that can affect your and your child's quality of life and are preventable. Type 1 diabetes is an autoimmune disease that has a strong genetic component, and it usually presents in childhood. Type 2 diabetes usually occurs later in life, but recently it has been on the rise. It is caused primarily by lifestyle factors, and patients are getting diagnosed at a younger age. Lifestyle factors include high blood pressure, overweight or obesity, insufficient physical activity, poor diet, and fat stored in the waist.

The definition of poor diet is where most mis-understanding and misinformation begins. What is a poor diet? Too much meat? Too much fat? Not enough vegetables?

Most functional physicians, many nurse practitioners, and a great number of health coaches (like me) have reviewed the data and formed a conclusion. The one commonality that drives a poor diet is excess sugar.

When people think of "obese," they usually associate it with eating too much fat. But fat is not the enemy. Healthy fats such as unrefined oils and avocados are nutritious and have numerous health benefits. But, instead of eating healthy fats and minimizing sugar, many people fall for the "diet soda" or "low-fat food" craze. When tasty fats are removed, companies replace them with fillers and sweeteners (refined or artificial).

At best, artificial sweeteners can make you consume a high quantity of foods with low nutritive value, and worse, they can contribute to metabolic disorders.

Many people add refined sugar to their coffee regularly. In fact, it is the consumption of sugar (not fat) that leads to fatty liver. When Remy was in the NICU, he developed fatty liver/hepatic steatosis, not because of my breast milk, but because of the sucrose he was being given regularly. Remy has a fatty liver due to the fructose he cannot metabolize. He is at a healthy weight and has no cavities because he does not eat sugar. But even people without an inherited error of metabolism can overload their livers with sugars. Much like alcoholism, sugar addiction will destroy hepatic cells over time and lead to liver disease.

Some people avoid "sweets" such as cookies and cakes but, instead, eat high amounts of fruits. While fruit has many vitamins and minerals, eating an excess of fruit can overload the liver with fructose. Fructose is the only sugar that is completely metabolized by the liver. While eating some fruit is healthy, too much of a good thing *contributes to fatty liver, insulin resistance, and other complications.*

My advice is to be kind to your liver and limit sugar. Eat more protein, eat healthy fats, and eat more vegetables than fruits. Above all, listen to your body. It doesn't lie. If you want to learn more about how elimination diets put my and my daughter's autoimmune disease into remission, read my book **You Are What You DON'T Eat: How elimination diets saved my son's life, allowed me to reclaim mine, and empowered my daughter to change the course of hers.**

Remy, age 6 (all dressed up and so many places to go)

Acknowledgements

Thank you to my husband, Shane, for putting our family above all else.

Thank you to my mom, Jennifer, for being with me during the hardest days.

Thank you to my daughter, Rebecca, for being the best sister to Remy.

Thank you to my dad, Warren, for instilling my passion for spreadsheets and statistics.

Thank you to my son, Remy, for showing me what bravery looks like and for forcing me to become a better chef.

Thank you to Courtney and all the other incredible NICU nurses who take care of the tiniest humans.

Thank you to Dr. Searle, Dr. Hernandez, and Dr. Perszyk for collectively saving my son's life.

ABOUT THE AUTHOR

Stefanie Billette is an educator, mother of two, and an agent of change. She earned a B.S. in Psychology with an Economics minor from the University of Richmond and a Master of Science in Management from the University of Florida's Warrington College of Business. Stefanie taught middle school, high school, and college for fifteen years. She is an ACE Certified Health Coach and Fitness Nutrition Specialist. Over the past decade, she has written articles about health and medicine and has coached those with autoimmune disease to manage their symptoms through nutrition therapy. Stefanie has published two other books: *The Adventures of Gona and Sierra: Silly Smoothie* and *You are What You DON'T Eat.*

Made in the USA
Columbia, SC
07 May 2025

57639106R00059